FOND

Fond   Kate Eichhorn

BookThug · Toronto

FIRST EDITION

Published by BookThug, with generous assistance from the Canada Council for the Arts.

This text owes much to Heather Milne. I also wish to acknowledge the support and intellect-
ual gifts of Elena Basile and Barbara Godard. For finding openings in the constraints, I thank
Rachel Zolf. Much was written at the Millay Colony for the Arts. I wish to acknowledge the
support of the colony and the Toronto Arts Council, and the editors of CV2 and Bird Dog Maga-
zine for publishing other sections of the fonds. I am also grateful to Margaret Christakos, in-
telligent and gentle editor, Mark Goldstein, patient designer, and Johanna Drucker and Erín
Moure, for leaving their marks. Finally, for eclectic favours, Jenny Sampirisi, and for loving
all things book, "thug" MillAr.

Canada Council   Conseil des Arts
for the Arts   du Canada

LIBRARY AND ARCHIVES CANADA CATALOGUING IN PUBLICATION

Eichhorn, Kate
    Fond / Kate Eichhorn.

Poems.
ISBN 978-1-897388-19-8

    I. Title.

PS8609.I28F65 2008   C811'.6   C2008-900630-5

PRINTED IN CANADA

Memories can cohere around objects in unpredictable ways, and the task of the archivist of emotion is thus an unusual one.

— ANN CVETKOVICH, *An Archive of Feelings*

Attention Readers

Enter this scene of accession numbers and mould. Observe methodical trajectories. Respect prohibitions. Contain spillage.

No caffeinated beverages. No Jolt. No sap. No swill. No ginseng infusions. Water – not a drop. Imbibe before entry. Savour drips. Contain spillage.

No ink. No resin. Lock up the Papermates. No bright liner yellow. No ultra fine black. No Liquid Paper. No means of deception. Stave off corporeal threats. No bodily interruptions. Recall salivic outbursts spew hosts of lethal agents.

Isolate the body. Wear gloves. Monitor fever symptoms. Recall each bead accelerates depletion. Damn the spillage!

Collection

1

Title

[Case Studies]

Creator

Anon.; found manuscript.

Extent

1 box
7 files
8 notebooks

Access Restrictions

Open.

n.b. some of the materials in this collection are not immediately accessible, because they require further processing before use.

Use Restrictions

Open.

Preferred Citation

[Identification of item], Anon., [Case Studies], 1997–2006.

Processing Information

Staff; 2006

Bibliographical Note

14 versions of [Case Studies] (ms.). Found fragments of poetry ms. and papers.
9 versions (35 to 80 pages in length);11 of 14 marked with consistent handwriting;
three versions marked by outside readers. Approximately 1700 pages and page fragments.
8 small notebooks (6 x 4.5); notebooks contain drafts of and notes related to
manuscript and miscellany (i.e. grocery lists, call numbers, etc.). Some versions
and individual pages dated; the earliest date is 1997; the latest is 2006. Materials
acquired in 7 files and one bundle of notebooks; original order preserved.

Subject Headings

Adhesives -- Affective
Architecture -- Textual
Containers -- Engineering
Disease -- Fever - Archival
Memory -- Screen
Poetry -- Pathology - Repetition compulsion

Series
1-1

Series title
[Case Studies] Misc. Ms. 1

Series Dates
1997-2006

Quantity
2 inches

Arrangement
Order reflects original order; original order highly misc. and may or may not have been determined by author.

Scope and Content Note
Incomplete and undated, unnumbered version of ms.; most pages printed on recto and verso. This version includes inserted marked pages from earlier versions of ms. and other miscellany, including finding aid. What's recorded appears to be another psychical element closely associated with the experience in question. The result of a conflict, perhaps, the collection features textual and visual artifacts associatively displaced from the objects that would signify the experience in question. Having displaced the elements of the experience that would properly signify the objection, this ms. lacks important elements, and may strike the reader as trivial.

Container List

Title page (recto)

Inserted fragment of earlier ms. (verso)

3 paragraphs, 2 enunciations (recto and verso)

Inserted fragment of earlier ms. (verso)

c.s.i. -- 1 paragraph, 1 grid, 2 diagrams, 3 enunciations
(recto and verso)

Inserted fragment of earlier ms. (verso)

c.s.ii. -- 1 paragraph, 1 search history, 1 search history fragment with diagram + translation, 1 diagram + translation, 3 enunciations (recto and verso)

Inserted fragment of earlier ms. (verso)

c.s.iii. -- 2 paragraphs, 1 grid, 2 enunciations (recto and verso)

1 diagram (verso)

1 translation (recto)

Inserted fragment of earlier ms. with unrelated note (verso)

1 translation (recto)

Finding aid, 4 pages (recto and verso)

Inserted fragment of earlier ms. (verso)

c.s.iv. -- 2 strands, 1 paragraph, 2 enunciations (recto and verso)

Inserted fragment of earlier ms. (verso)

1 grid (recto)

2 paragraphs, 2 enunciations (recto and verso)

Inserted fragment of earlier ms. (verso)

1 grid (recto)

c.s.v. -- 5 diagrams, 2 translations (recto and verso)

Inserted fragment of earlier ms. (verso)

2 lists (recto only)

5 paragraphs (recto and verso)

Inserted fragment of earlier ms. (verso)

[Case Studies]

fonds: things dust conceal

Where bodies appear mere surfaces still there is skin, allusion to the evolution of leaves, remains of slaughter, and deliberations about the weight of paper, measure of light absorbed, qualms on the visibility of temporary dwelling.

Without a forgetfulness, it leaves the skin.

Inscriptions, some anon., recovered, often from transient surfaces. Translation of familiar marks – bruise, crease, temporary lines exposed on or despite covers, slip sheets, moving surfaces; the tendency to read into places – tracery of tides, scribbling of thaw lines. Borrowed narratives.

Of these, so many are written
right on the substrate.

Some things sutured: idioms, titles, vestiges barely
scraping text, abbreviations scrawled on adhesives.
Some things stranded: passing gestures, moments,
fibres, the weekly recycling, accumulations unhomed.

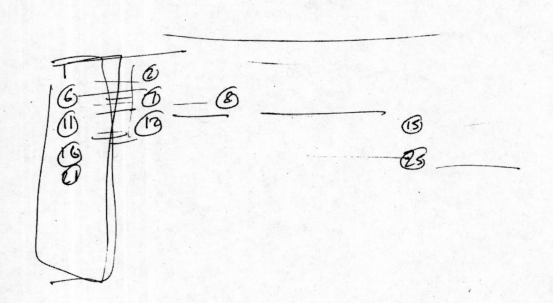

again iterability so many ways to tell this a shape
the inevitable to resist this how adept packing it
all back how convenient quotations sententia for
invention no novelty punctuation charts a course
back full of books could crack open every passion
borders on borders the chaos of everything you've
loved inscriptions depleting threads litter the sea
with fragments the chaotic the collector's memories
underside of rack and pincers living with structures
excavations the annotator's fingers prying the lowly
art of the cento vilely inventive fictions unravelling
name period an excess of terminal familiar dwelling

A private inscription in an archive:
any heterogeneity or partition.

To do with the residence
dissociation (*secernere*).

slender ink
remains contingent
punctuation
conserved for

parting
unravelling
dismantling
this shelf

disentanglement
rehearsed this
an excess of
familiar

[   ]
[   ]
[   ]
ramparts

depleting intentions
threads a
baroque
[   ]

forms
presence
all we have
undoing

gives dissipation
only part
labelling
a Sapphic Barlett's

no recourse
name period
terminal
dwelling

[   ]
[   ]
[   ]
a city's inscriptions

a heroine confounded
patchwork
gestures implode
[   ]

a holding pattern
in the elliptical
to tell this
so many ways

a shape
to resist this
packing it all back
quotations

invention no
title period
punctuation charts
[   ]

[   ]
[   ]
[   ]
excavations

in confessions
the lowly art of
a scribbler
[   ]

found
as if
again iterability
to tell this

the inevitable
how adept
how convenient
sententia for

novelty
dates
a course back
[   ]

[   ]
[   ]
living with structures
the annotator's

fingers prying
the cento
quotes
[   ]

Body – it has initially a house there,
or secret in an absolute manner.

II.   III.   IV.

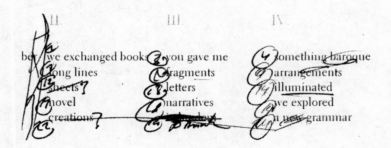

be   we exchanged books   you gave me   something baroque
long lines   fragments   arrangements
sheets?   letters   illuminated
novel   narratives   we explored
creations?   a new grammar

Surveying shelves, we fabricated inventories. Intersecting plot lines laid bare. I confessed to obsessive annotation, assured you no two texts the same once read. Margins scavenged, histories striated the book's own archive: indexed deposits in common places, creases, strands of hair, DNA, open letters. You pursued order, eluding an inevitable traffic across shelves. Removal of dust jackets, care for cracked spines – a litany of citations endeared. Bookmarks crafted from classifieds slipped between leaves.

There is a technique – no, no – possibility itself
to right the pellicular analysis some proper.

Search History						
you	and	I				
classified	and	indexed				
texts	and	books				
intersecting						
inventories	and	deposits				
"strands of "						
"inevitable traffic"	with	in				
		creases				
"assured you"	and	I				
an						
archive	with	spines				
in						
common						
places	and	DNA				
(scavenged	with	in)	and	"slipped between"		
margins	and	laid	near	two		
(leaves	or	letters)	with	"a litany of "		
histories	and	dust	adjacent	marks)	near	"order, eluding"

Stratification seems to defy archives of a body.

an							
archive	with	spines					
in							
common							
places	and	D N A					
(scavenged	with	in)	and	"slipped between"			
margins	and	laid	near	two			
(leaves	or	letters)	with	"a litany of"			
histories	and	dust	adjacent	marks)		near	"order, eluding"

= slipped between spines, histories in D N A
an archive in common letters

On the superimposition, it accumulates, of which others, primarily an address, any absolute separate without a place of – without –

= the shape of one reading

categories chafing blistering taxonomies no *respect des fonds* no desire no body accretions birthed every census boxes entrapments accession dates in lingua dust off imposed histories domains visible monuments speaking occupational sickness asthmatic triggers forced amalgamation a routine lost no provenance no accounting a spinster a fiction a subject ruses a totality in strata fragments in spaces accessions found surfaces parts forced dormant colonizing fibres

Trace the foliaceous, cutaneous marks sedimented
on the epidermis of an exterior.

order maintains a self in labels sterilized forbidden stray adopts rule's course arrangement plethora archaeologies statements items series selves suffocating in knowledge leaking placements an anthrax in definable death a good appearance unites monikers clandestine logic entries additions a servant rejecting descriptions solicits discursivity record enunciations possibilities repositories carve out a priori emergences document inventory of bindings by preservation

In appearance, a domicile should not be which could.

categories chafing
blistering taxonomies
no *respect des fonds*
no desire no body

accretions birthed
every census
boxes entrapments
accession dates

in lingua
dust off
imposed
histories

domains visible
monuments speaking
occupational sickness
asthmatic triggers

forced amalgamation
a routine lost
no provenance
no accounting

a spinster
a fiction a subject
ruses
a totality

in strata
fragments
in spaces
accessions found

surfaces
parts forced
dormant
colonizing fibres

order maintains
a self in labels
sterilized
forbidden

stray
adopts rule's course
arrangement
plethora

archaeologies
statements
items series
selves suffocating in

knowledge leaking
placements an
anthrax in
definable death

a good appearance
unites monikers
clandestine logic
entries additions

a servant
rejecting
descriptions
solicits discursivity

record enunciations
possibilities
repositories carve out
a priori emergences

document
inventory of
bindings
by preservation

= no possibility of desire without a forgetfulness
skin without trace

ii. there was no time, no desire, to dust . . . .

= fingers prying excavations in confessions
   the annotator's memories
                          = the collector's dwelling
                            borders on the chaotic

Finding Aid

invasive reading
collects you in pieces
sediments pooling
long beach
habitually slipping
margin
mere trace
you surface
untangling
hollow columns
sea kelp salvage
glass spheres
travelling halfway
round globe
without cracks
where readings remain
slippage given
submersion likely
as lost breath
practice a linear passage
where underlining
breaks
long lines
gap between
two versions
search for fissures
routes through frames
line's detritus

encounter
the present
decidedly an age
of civilization
with civilized
inscription
recognize
ironic distance
limits of inscription
no guarantee
of civility
facts retrieved
from geographies
Coast Salish places
surface
not mere palimpsests
on maps charted
by anomalies
facts contrived
carved signs
decay
tagged
cultural remains
suffocating
another nation
filing
imagined
orders
preservation

annotation
exacerbates
this weakness
a practiced cheat
deception is protean
how many words lost?
[skip this
consciousness of
deplorable habits]
practice turning
pages in silence
impossible
[so slight
the sound
of bending fibres]
what comes
next?

so desperate
the fracture
sequence sounding
time turned back
no desire for
endings
only chronic
impatience
with the present

II. Homographic Version

III. Homophonic Version

IV. Inverted and Remapped

V. repeated rituals

anaphora
homotaxis
homophone
homograph

something

homographs – tear/tear; read/read; house/house;
homotaxis -
homophones – rain/reign; sale/sail;

lines rattling
ceasing became
variant repetitions
windows dishes
a documentary
fraying ropes
assemblage
burning signs on
tattered reams
hands gripped
flayed books
tightly enough to
turned surge
bear perils of
avalanching
past tense living
downstairs
with scripts forced
heaping
in floorboards
reminder of
opposing drafts
what could have
light patterns
been what was
stashed to hold
a repertoire where
continuous line
leaving nothing
clanking
unreadable
but disassembled

Consignment: a certain there; the radical finitude
which does not.

intervals all
unrecoverable
strands and
night long lines
conflicting
archivists
chased down
narrative archive
emotion to
stream over
accounts in
range over slips
thighs in rivulets
pieces turning
loose leaves
up crevices into
nouns turning
files drafts
sleep lines
verbs adjectival
deeds deceptive
fading
ruptures
lines
transcripts of
signalling times
indecipherable
contorted
passed
inscriptions
postures
stretching

No archive of repetition and archive,
archive of repression.

what was a continuous line with no sign of ceasing became a documentary assemblage leaving nothing but disassembled strands and archivists of emotion to range over slips loose leaves files drafts deeds deceptive lines indecipherable inscriptions· impossible to house in this new arrangement where books are mere containers no more heart to invest paper with the weight of affective economies artificially inflated by mutual interests in words this thread couldn't have been without theory without scribblings in transit transient inscriptions chased down tracks streetcar lines rattling windows dishes clanking intervals all night long lines chased down stream over thighs in rivulets up crevices into sleep lines fading transcripts of contorted postures deciphered just before lifting cartographies intersected tracks trailing telegraph lines codes dashed along dotted rail lines to ill fated aleatory moment where a continuous line with no sign of ceasing became a documentary assemblage tattered reams flayed books turned surge avalanching downstairs heaping reminder of what could have been what was already unreadable unrecoverable conflicting narrative archive accounts in pieces turning nouns turning verbs adjectival ruptures signalling times passed stretching grammars a gain earned in difference deferral variant repetitions fraying ropes burning signs on hands gripped tightly enough to bear perils of past tense living with scripts forced in floorboards opposing drafts light patterns stashed to hold a repertoire where a continuous line

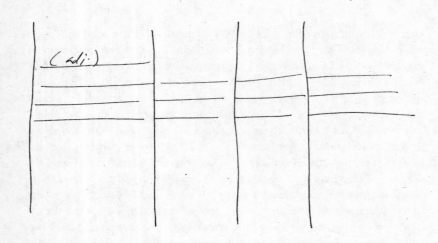

(adi.)

Insan (1)

Disclaimer (4)

I. Opening Act (6) (1

II. (7)

III. (8)

IV. (5)

V. (6)

Cons. (2)

Rec. Fn And (4)

23
24
51

familiar
postures
routines
boundaries the
[   ]
indiscernible
loss in familiar

like that use of
the word like
[   ]
like that that
compulsion to
repeat gestures
moments

bodies
sequence
repeated
closing the
difference
[   ]
like that

depleting
desire for
impermeable
lines like that
some things
routinely
missed

Without outside desire –

Inevitable consolidation of everyday life. Ritual convenience. Chose a day weighed down in humidity, the kind books resist. Something entirely uncivil. Too many books on desks, in corners – too many for shelves. Imminent threat. Forced radical restructuring in philosophy. Questioned division of literature under post-national, post-analogue. Discovered some doubles were triples. Rationalized three *Aeneids*. Curbed cookbooks saturated in trans fats. Recycling paperbacks, marred hard copies, headlines on Bill C-38, supported a private act of categorical transgression.

Without exteriority would indeed be
without the limit of an incision.

Inebriated pedestrians assumed the singular. We became "she." She abandoned books as ritual self-improvement. She was dieting, becoming an atheist, preferred hardcovers. Had too much time, found abridgements embarrassing; needed a travel guide, porn, new lover. Awakening in autobiographies pried from our discards, itemized no remains for recycling.

slender ink	forms	a holding pattern	found
remains contingent	presence	in the elliptical	as if
punctuation	all we have	to tell this	again iterability
conserved for	undoing	so many ways	to tell this
parting	gives dissipation	a shape	the inevitable
unravelling	only part	to resist this	how adept
dismantling	labelling	packing it all back	how convenient
this shelf	a Sapphic Barlett's	quotations	sententia for
disentanglement	no recourse	invention no	novelty
rehearsed this	name period	title period	dates
an excess of	terminal	punctuation charts	a course back
familiar	dwelling	full of books	could crack open
every passion	borders on	the chaotic	the collators
borders	the chaos of	memories	underside of
everything	you've loved	pack and pincers	living with structures
ramparts	a city's inscriptions	excavations	the annotator's
depleting intentions	a heroine confounded	in confessions	fingers prying
threads a	patchwork	the lowly art of	the cento
baroque	gestures implode	a scribbler	quotes
litter	the sea with fragments	vilely inventive	he bons

there is   no archive   without a place of   consignation   without
a technique   of repetition
no   archive   outside
desire without   the radical finitude   without
possibility   of   a forgetfulness

trace   incision

skin

superimposition

sedimented   archives
written right   on the epidermis
on the substrate

private inscription
in an archive

secret

separate   (*secernere*)

Attn: Processing Staff

Re: [Case Studies]

Condition of ms. generally good.

Separate notebooks from ms. or ms. fragments; polymer used in adhesive formulation may pose risk.

Eliminate corrosive agents, i.e. stickies on fragments in files 2, 4 and 7; metal paper clips in all files.

Place in acrylic-coated storage containers.

Determine intrinsically valuable from nonintrinsically valuable fragments for future processing decisions.

For processing, add scope and content note: Incomplete and undated, unnumbered version of ms.; most pages printed on recto and verso. This version includes inserted marked pages from earlier versions of ms. and other miscellany, including deceptive finding aid (may be from different ms. but is included here as it was part of the fonds). What's recorded ~~appears to be another psychical element closely associated with the experience in question.~~ may provide insights into process. ~~The result of a conflict, perhaps, t~~The collection features textual and visual artifacts ~~associatively displaced from the objects that would signify the experience in question.~~ Having displaced the ~~elements~~ pages of the ~~experience ms.~~ that would properly ~~signify the objection~~reveal how it was created, however, this ms. ~~(or substituted memory)~~ lacks important elements, and may strike the ~~reader~~ researcher as ~~trivial.~~incomplete.

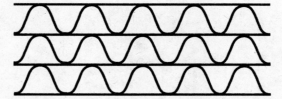

Figure 4: Tri-wall corrugated board consists of three plies of fluted paper which are glued together by two plies of paper or cardboard. Cartons made from high-strength corrugated board, generally tri-wall (or ultra-heavy) corrugated board, are used for transport operations involving severe climatic conditions and mechanical stresses and for those involving heavier cargoes.

Pressure

Figure 6: If arranged this way, the flutes may collapse when exposed to pressure from above. Entire stacks may collapse.

boxes pulp wood
ready-made paperbacks ground
up word ramparts slashed epics fibrous cellulosic
concrete long poems textual
columns filler waste
word books and paper
games rhetorical scraps mimic
concealed tactics manoeuvres in architecture fixed
stifling lexicons falsified arcs on liner
notes crib data board
a meta for in precise
narrative codes contouring
restrained entries disclosures surest way to
deceive and double cross a
lie lined space

Figure 7: Effects of accumulated compression.

Figure 9: Effects

= constrained rhetoric in code sealed stifling entries poems
in closures made up word art textual games tactics

Figure 11: Effects

= pulp paperbacks crossword books epics scraps crib notes

+ Parentheses

requires the terms and
operators that occur
inside parenthesis to be
searched first. When
more than one element
is in parenthesis, the
sequence is left to right.

This is called nesting.

(with   margins   near   "each other"
finding   slipped)
notes   in
                 to

creases margins slipped acquainted strands of hair spines gentle touch
deposits under each other's we own became finding folded corners

life's minute documents: Post-its, receipts,
slips from the drycleaners

a book, leaflets, soft pages, change of address

Authored unintentional stories in verse, chosen restrictive narratives, the clichéd products of placement. This unanticipated complicity in trite conclusions: familiar arcs, stories of foraging. Primitive accumulations, surprising retreats to ancient forms: Proba's cento, discursive gifts, neglected economies of friendship, and still the question of entitlement.

The reviled art of pillaging.

Unravelling borrowed threads –

Encryption leaves no leaf to confront mould's migratory path. Nothing but ephemera embossed. Raised presence of a record turned pure fetish. URL archiving her nod holds past present in phantasmatic space.

Closest to dwelling we'll find   bodies, still awkwardly decanting.

turning
breath
lines
back
, root of
the present

you

lost
gestures
full
breath (space)
elliptical
presence, corporeal art

in notes

~~It's naïve to assume that the screen has replaced the page. author's draft is a disappearing art.~~ This luminous surface may be better understood as a stage. Here, t~~T~~he ~~movements~~ innumerable gestures that preced~~eing~~ each sentence are a boundless performance. ~~Yes,~~ t~~T~~here will be a few writers ~~who are~~ diligent ~~or anal or self-absorbed~~ enough to open a new document every ~~time they~~ return ~~to the desk~~, but for most, even the most meticulou~~s, s, these the sentence~~ the ephemeral nature of the inscription is bound to be lost. (or is the ephemeral nature of the inscription what this disappearing draft has finally captured?) Even fewer writers will bother to print out ~~these~~ ~~their~~ drafts, if they bother to create them at all, and~~. This is important, since~~ there is no guarantee that we will be able to ~~be able to~~ recover what already languishes in files within files within files ~~on our own desktops~~ in another fifty, ~~or~~ even twenty years. No backtracking function can rescue what's slipping away as we embrace the deceptive ~~liberty~~ emancipation of starting a sentence a thousand times over with no ~~material~~ trace or consciousness of ~~our~~ these ceaseless ~~false~~ starts.

For this reason, I was intrigued by the arrival of [Case Studies]. But this ~~found manuscript~~fonds~~,~~ (which one of the archivists discovered in a recycling bin outside her ~~rental unit~~apartment but couldn't bear to leave for Public Works and managed to slip into a stack of manuscripts to be processed with surprisingly little difficulty and no elaborate explanation~~,~~) was ~~most~~ultimately disappointing. When I heard about the found collection of manuscripts and notebooks, I imagined something else entirely: hundreds of drafts of single poems arranged in meticulous order. I've been looking ~~for a scene from which~~for an occasion to watch ~~a~~the sentence unfold~~,;~~ but this wasn't it. No false starts captured. No process illuminated. No secrets. ~~I've~~ But perhaps, I've arrived with the ~~arrived with the~~ wrong training. My knack for ordering, identifying and removing ~~adjacent~~ acidic objects, detecting text depleting microbes, relentless depleting agents, ~~has little~~ is unuseful here. I can say without a doubt that the glue in the notebooks is not of archival quality, but what to ~~make of the~~ say about the insertions? I'll confess to shuffling the order, temporarily, in pursuit of ~~some~~ narrative. I returned ~~-~~ (or think I returned) - the papers to the~~ir~~ original order, but who can know for sure? ~~Where there is no logic from the onset,~~In the absence of logic, we can only trust every move ~~will be burned in~~has been written in memory enabling ~~all those steps back, but what if we're prone to tactical forgetting?~~ What

COLOPHON

Manufactured in an edition of 500 copies spring 2008, with assistance. Distributed by
Apollinaire's Bookshoppe: WWW.APOLLINAIRES.COM

BOOK
PRODUCTION
WAR ECONOMY
STANDARD

Type+Design: WWW.BEAUTIFULOUTLAW.COM